Pahelu Paanu

A Collection of First Pages
of Pathshala Magazine

Written by
A. Pradyumnasuri M.S.
Disciple of
Gacchnayak A. Hemchandrasuriji M.S.

English Translation by
S. Pararthyashashreeji M.S.
Disciple of
S. Praveena-Daxyasha-Dhrutiyasha-Deeprayasha-
Drushtiyasha-Shreeji M.S.

INDIA · SINGAPORE · MALAYSIA

ISBN 979-8-89186-854-0

Shasansamrat Acharya Vijay Nemisuriswarji Maharaj

Acharya Vijay
Chandrodaysuriswarji
Maharaj

Acharya Vijay
Ashokchandrasuriswarji
Maharaj

Acharya Vijay
Pradyumnasuriswarji
Maharaj

Acharya Vijay
Somchandrasuriswarji Maharaj

Appreciative Contributor
Inspired by Panyas Shrutchandra Vijayji M.S.,
Mr Kushal Shaileshbhai Kothari
Ms Dhanvi Rakeshbhai Kothari
Sushilaben Kothari Parivaar – Walkeshwar, Mumbai

In the memory of Late Manoben Chotalal Anandji Parekh
Mrs Muktaben Manharbhai Parekh – Atlanta USA

Contents

Preface

**Now it's up to You,
Now it's up to Rain and Soil**

Thoughts hold significant power in shaping our lives, whether they are positive or negative, as they deeply influence our personalities.

Generally, all positive determination, perception and thinking signifies the grace of lord.

Ilbusca

Each page will reveal new dimension to cultivate virtues and will lessen thoughts of vice. Everyone appreciates the best. As you focus on the positive, the meritorious you will become, ready to blossom. The musings and fresh perspectives within each page of the Pathshala magazine reflect this transformation. By such reflection I have sowed the seeds of faith that will bloom. The response from enthusiastic readers and their letters of appreciation for my thought-provoking writing on the first page has been overwhelming.

'First page is the heart of the magazine.'
'First page transformed my life.'
*'I really appreciate your article, **"Bridging the Gap between Understanding and Behavior."'***
'I have read your articles many times and have by hearted the one I liked.'

These were the feedback from the readers. One reader also praised by saying; "Your magazine offers exceptional content, but the first page stands out, reflecting your profound vision of life."

After seeing and learning the heart of our readers, on their demand, whatever I have gained by the grace of lord, I have just shared it. I have sowed the seeds, now it is up to the rain and soil.

I have given my best, now it is up to you! The poetic line of the poet, Makrand Dave conveys my meaning, hence, it is the title!

– Vijay Pradyumna Suriji

Translator's Note

We are truly fortunate to possess the ability to convey our gratitude and the sensitivity and intelligence required to experience kindness as human beings. None of us can claim to be entirely "self-made." We acknowledge and express our gratitude to those individuals who have played a pivotal role in shaping us, instilling essential values, cultivating crucial habits, bestowing unique abilities, and honing our interpersonal skills.

This remarkable journey has been made possible through the blessings of Param Pujya Acharya Shri Nemisuri M.S. and Acharya Shri Somchandrasuri M.S. I seize this moment to extend my heartfelt gratitude to Gacchnayak Hemchandrasuriji M.S. for his unwavering inspiration and support. I am equally thankful to my Guruji, Drashtiyashashriji M.S., who stood by me during both my highs and lows. I also want to express my gratitude to Param Pujya Acharya Rajhanssuriji M.S., a disciple of Acharya Pradyumnasuriji M.S. for his gracious permission to collaborate on this book.

I would also like to express my deep appreciation to Chirag, Shruti, Shripal, Darsh and Arpita for their invaluable assistance in every possible way.

Furthermore, I cannot overlook the immense insights and profound clarity I gained through Acharya Shri Pradhyumansuriji M.S.'s work 'Pahelu Paanu.' Each page of his words contained the essence of wisdom, akin to the meticulously unwrapped treasure of a priceless gift.

"Pahelu Paanu" offers a comprehensive guide, encompassing self-destructive tendencies that disrupt our inner peace, techniques for profound self-analysis, a spirit of amicability toward the entire universe, and an attitude of composure in all circumstances.

Through "Pahelu Paanu," I acquired a deeper understanding of various aspects, such as the significance of valuing the rare, the bridging of the gap between understanding and action, the clarity that purpose lends to life, and the realization that by conquering our minds, we can conquer the world.

હૈયાનો હોંકારો

Inner Voice

When you are completely aligned with your work, it gradually speaks to your inner self and guides you further. Sometimes you may hear words of inspiration and motivation that further fuel your passion. Additionally, when you complete a task beautifully, you may receive well-deserved words of recognition and appreciation.

Clear Your Mind,
And Happiness Will Follow!

Empty your cup. A full cup cannot accept anything more.

It is a universal law that when we fill a container, it becomes full. We take pleasure in observing a vase or a basket brimming with flowers, for emptiness is not a pleasing sight. However, behold, the mind is a peculiar thing. If you leave it empty, happiness shall spring forth from it of it' s own accord.

Tammy Carrick

We fill our minds with the countless good thoughts and expect joy to arise from it. This may indeed be true, but alongside the good, the bad thoughts also creep in, bring it forth a tempest. And so our joy becomes like vapor, bound to dissipate.

Therefore, keep your mind like a clean slate, so the happiness maybe experienced. Dhyan, the state of meditation, is defined as a "Vacant state of mind". "ध्यानं निर्विषयं मन:!" Dhyan is blissful, and it keeps the mind calm and transparent. It requires effort and intentionality. When the mind is free of any thought for a definite period, all the bounds of the world and physical existence resolve naturally. It is the greatest game, for it requires no action, and yet you emerge victorious.

If you do not think, you do not speak; If you do not speak, you do not act. All the three aspects wither away. The more you keep your mind free of any thoughts, the stronger it becomes. And a strong mind is a force unto itself.

You can win it, if you do not allow even a single thought to enter your mind. If you succeed in this endeavor, you will have fulfilled the ancient adage; 'How to win the world? Win it through your mind.' "जगत् जीतं केन! मनो येन!"

Every individual may have their own limitations in winning their mind, but if you have a strong desire to remain ever joyful and in a state of bliss, you can achieve it. Monks and seekers are always striving to maintain a vacant state of mind. Let us also enroll ourselves in this class, and with firm determination, train our minds for peace.

Mind Engaged in Work is Fruitful

Pujya Acharya Maharaj Shree Dhurandhar Suri Ji lived a life that was true to the title given above. He preached and practiced the same philosophy, constantly engaging himself in positive activities, as he believed that an idle mind invites destruction, while engaging in good deeds brings positive results.

Acharya Shree was always engrossed in reading and writing of scriptures, shlokas, and gathas, taking notes of all the good points and thoughts that he came across. His handwriting was so beautiful that readers would want to read it again and again. He authored several books, including Barsa-Sutra and Uttradhyan Sutra, showcasing his artistic and literary talent.

Even during his battle with cancer, Acharya Shree remained engaged in his work, spending sleepless nights simplifying each verse (Shloka) of Shri Bhaktamar. He would muse on each gatha, paraphrase it, and compose rhythms related to the meaning. Sometimes, he even composed two songs (stavan) from the same gatha to make it easier. He believed in the saying, "When all mortals are asleep, only penance practitioners are awake."

Acharya Shree's mind was always pure and full of good feelings towards others, making him immune to physical pain. He had developed self-discipline through strong practice and never allowed his mind to be idle. Even while conversing with others, he would be thinking of creating something new. He was a true winner of his mind through his self-discipline and was a great example to all who seek to live a fulfilling and productive life.

પુણ્ય આંગળિયાત છે, માલિક તો ગુણ છે

Virtue is the Master,
Punya follows the Master

It is a common desire among human beings to seek happiness and pleasure in life. Many people believe that happiness can only be attained by obtaining the things they desire such as material possessions, relationships, and ideal circumstances. However, there is another important aspect that should not be overlooked - the doctrine of welfare.

Following virtue and doing good deeds will naturally lead to happiness and well-being. By developing a strong attraction towards virtue, one can attract positive karmic matter or punya which results in a peaceful and happy life. Generosity, for instance, is a virtue that leads to charity, and charity brings punya. The example of Shalibhadra illustrates the rewards of selfless service and charitable acts.

However, it is unfortunate that many people only desire the fruits of punya but do not want to engage in the actions that bring it. It is important to develop a strong attraction towards virtues such as charity, mercy, and goodness. By doing so, we can become better human beings and experience true fulfilment in life. Remember, happiness is a byproduct of virtuous actions, so focus on cultivating virtue and the rest will follow naturally.

વહેતા પાણીમાં હાથ ધોવાનું કામ કરીએ
Embrace the Power of Doing Good

Strive to do good deeds whenever, wherever, and to whomever possible. If you consider yourself intelligent, take a pen and a book and note down the services you have received from others. You are likely pleased by many people around you. Now, consider how much you have served or helped others. How many have been pleased by your kind help? This comparison will clearly point out that we are often more interested in receiving than giving back.

Before you go to sleep, think about whether you have been useful to anyone. If you prefer to do so, there are many opportunities to help others. For example, you can assist an elderly person or someone with a disability to cross the road. Or, if you see a student with a broken bicycle rushing to an examination center while you are riding a scooter, you can help them by zipping up their school bag, giving them a lift, and ensuring they arrive on time. You may also help a load puller find the right address. Just a simple act of kindness can bring a smile to someone's face and courage to their heart.

They will be full of gratitude and wish you

well. This is your real profit, a countless treasure that is more valuable than money. So, will you perform such genuine acts of kindness?

Help those around you!

Exercise Your Firmness
With Discretion

One of the positive aspects of the human mind is that it can be cultivated, nurtured, trained, and developed in the way we want it to be. However, the human ego is deeply rooted, and its repercussions can be felt in multiple ways. As a result, a person can become obstinate in every matter, insisting on their own beliefs and demands, and imposing them on others, even if they aren't the only truth. This insistence can be good if it's used to follow virtuous rules of life, but if it's otherwise, it can be harmful.

A person who is persistent in minor or small issues often becomes a loser when it comes to life-saving rules. This insistence on minor matters can cause serious damage that cannot be regained. Even a so-called vice person can become stubborn in small matters. As the Hindi saying goes, "don't make small things a big issue, else you will turn small." This is the essence of wisdom. Real intelligence must be above obstinacy and open-mindedness is essential "बुद्धेर्फलमनाग्रहः"

Let me explain this with an example. Once a group of friends were passing by the road when they smelled a strong, sweet fragrance. One friend suggested that there must be a garden nearby, while another said it must be a lorry loaded with incense sticks passing by, and the third insisted that it was because a lady who had crossed the road was heavenly perfumed. The matter was turned and twisted into an issue, even though none of them had any proof to support their statements.

Instead of insisting on their own beliefs, they could have simply enjoyed the fragrance and said "Oh, you may be right." This would have resolved the matter without any argument. In conclusion, being open-minded and practical is more important than being obstinate.

Don't to be a Judge, Be a Witness

Why do humans have a bad habit of always wanting to share their opinion? If they meet someone, they are quick to judge and label them as good or bad. However, this habit of throwing our unsolicited opinions around is not only common but also worthless.

It's often said that advice is easily available, but it is truly valuable only when asked for. Unfortunately, many people fail to understand this simple fact and end up wasting their speech power on unwarranted judgments. Such behavior is highly dangerous and can lead to misunderstandings and conflicts.

We must strive to be objective and maintain a balanced approach by keeping a safe distance and not involving ourselves unnecessarily. Instead of being a judge, we must learn to be a witness. Once we develop the ability to witness events without getting attached to them, we will experience a significant difference. Life will become more comfortable and joyful.

To start, try being a witness for an hour. Observe objectively whatever happens around you without offering your opinion. By doing so, you'll realize that it's possible to keep our minds away from the impulse to judge. While it may be difficult to detach our soul from our body, we can still keep our minds at bay.

Remember, nothing is impossible if you're determined to succeed. With constant practice, you'll become wiser and better

at controlling your thoughts. Our minds are as delicate as flowers, and we can shape them as we wish. So, let's make a good beginning from today and cultivate the habit of being a witness rather than a judge.

Navigating the Perils of Flattery, Criticism, and Comparison

A discussion was underway on how to attain a state of mental calmness. One of the participants offered his view, "Oh, it is quite challenging to refrain from both praise and criticism and avoid comparisons." To this, the wise one responded, "Yes, we should indeed express genuine appreciation when we come across something praiseworthy, but it must not be driven by any selfish interest. On the other hand, we should steer clear of criticism at all costs. Often, our expressions of admiration are as insincere as when we say, 'Crow, your voice is sweet!' Can we really call that appreciation or is it merely flattery?" The fox praises the crow to get a loaf of bread, driven by its self-interest. Let us distinguish between genuine praise and flattery. Flattery is all about serving one's own purpose.

Likewise, our criticism is like the sour grapes that the fox decries. The fox, in its cunningness, rationalizes its failure to get grapes by claiming that they are sour. This is neither a reality nor a fact but merely a self-defense mechanism. Our mind becomes sullied and sinful when we engage in flattery or criticism.

Equally perilous is our tendency to compare things, events, and people. This inclination brings pain and suffering. If we can learn to let go of attachment and aversion, we can liberate ourselves from the agony of comparisons. Only then can we keep our mind free from any pain and impurities.

ફરિયાદઃ ઉત્તમતાની ઉણપમાંથી જન્મે છે

Complaints: The Result of Lack of Excellence

A fault-finding nature can hinder your personal development and lead to a habitual complaining mentality. By constantly complaining, you map out a road of pain for yourself. The truth is that we must change the things that are within our control and accept the things that are beyond our control without blaming others. This is the key to making progress in life.

To avoid complaining, we can either accept the situation or create a proper situation with cooperation and mutual understanding. Blaming others will only destroy your inner power, so it's important to avoid a negative approach. For example, when you begin learning Gujarati grammar, you are taught to turn subjective sentences into objective ones. Similarly, we must make our lives more upright and progressive by turning negative situations into positive ones.

Shelby Elizabeth

Let me share my own experience. When I first started giving sermons, only eight to ten members would attend. They would say, "Everybody is at home, eating good food and relaxing. They are not interested in attending sermons." But I took a positive approach and thought, "How nice it is that these few people are here! Let's create a great environment that everyone will want to attend." This approach yielded positive results and made my mind feel fresh and cheerful.

As human beings, we must keep negative thoughts at bay. Negativity is like rabies from a mad dog. We must be watchful and not allow it to consume us. Let us fill our inner worlds with fresh flowers and fragrances and avoid negativity at all costs.

Good Manners: The Foundation of a Fulfilling Life

Uttam is a compound word that comes from two Sanskrit words, Utt (up) and Tam (lower element). When you rise above the lower elements of your nature, you become uttam. At the center of the lower element lies ego, while rising above them requires selflessness and consideration for others. When you care for others, your manners become refined naturally.

For instance, when the Shraman Bhagavan Mahavir went out for alms on the day of parna, he avoided streets where he saw a single mendicant at the door of a house, and even left streets where he saw a squirrel drinking water or a dove picking corn. His compassion for all living beings was exemplary.

Similarly, when you see off a guest, it's considered courteous to close the door after they leave, as a sign of respect. These small gestures may seem insignificant, but they can have a profound impact on how others perceive you and how you perceive yourself.

Whether you're in a business meeting, sharing a meal, or entering a temple, maintaining a pleasant and courteous demeanor can go a long way in making life more fulfilling. Good manners and consideration for others can help build better relationships and a stronger sense of self.

Remember, we all have the potential to be extraordinary!

Debt Redemption

Each of us bears three types of debt: a paternal debt to honor our cultural heritage and values, a teacher's debt to repay their boundless contribution to our development, and a debt to the universe to be helpful to those around us. These debts must be consciously acknowledged and sincerely addressed throughout our lives.

To honor our parents' obligation, we must strive to live up to their values and traditions. While we cannot repay their debt, we can show our gratitude by preserving their legacy. Similarly, we owe a debt of gratitude to our teachers, whether they be schoolteachers, professors, or religious instructors. Our lives are enriched by their contributions, and it is our duty to pay it forward by being helpful to others.

For example, once a man was buying vegetables but found himself short by 20 rupees when it was time to pay. He was upset and unsure of what to do, but another buyer who witnessed this offered to pay the remaining amount. The relieved man asked for the other buyer's address to return the money, but the kind man refused, saying "No need to return the money. You too can help others in such a way." Acts of kindness like this are a way to redeem our debt and show gratitude for the blessings in our lives.

In conclusion, we urge our audience to reflect on their debts and strive to repay them through conscious efforts to be helpful and live up to the values and traditions passed down to us by our parents and teachers. Gratitude is a virtue that should be embraced and expressed through our actions towards others.

કોરી સીલેટના લીસોટા

Scribbles on a Blank Slate

A person's childhood can be compared to a blotting paper that immediately absorbs everything around them, leaving a lasting impact. A child's first sense, the visual sense, is incredibly sharp, and they observe everything that happens around them. These images are imprinted deeply into their minds, remaining intact forever, despite the countless other images generated subsequently.

This experience is common to us all, so it's important to continuously behave in a positive manner in front of children. Our behavior should be pleasant, our speech soft, and our interactions simple. The actions and behavior that a child observes have a profound impact on their mind.

The seeds of goodness that we plant in a child at an early age, with the nourishment of age and education, will flourish into a characteristic of good behavior with others in the future. Therefore, we must be careful about our behavior during a child's early years, as they are like the scribbles on a blank slate that will last forever.

Filtering Valuable Knowledge in the Information Age

Our minds are constantly bombarded with information from various sources, such as television, radio, newspapers, and the internet. It can be difficult to distinguish useful knowledge from useless information, like trying to separate gravel from wheat. To optimize our mental storage, we must be selective and only retain valuable content.

Think of our minds as a vault rather than a warehouse. Just as we keep precious gems in a vault and scraps in a warehouse, we should only hold onto the rare and valuable gems of knowledge. Let's cultivate an attitude of discernment and focus on enriching our lives with the glow of new insights.

સુખી થવાની સાદી ચાવી; અસતો માઁ સદ્ ગમય:

Simple key to happiness

Being a good human being requires effort and dedication. It's easy to behave well for a short period of time, but difficult to maintain it over time. To make it easier, there are three steps that can help: surrounding oneself with sacred company, reading sacred texts, and engaging in sacred behavior. In today's world, where falsehood and deception are rampant, meeting a righteous person is considered a blessing. Only when a person is graced by God do they have the chance to meet a righteous person who is like a sweet oasis amidst a salty ocean. By analyzing and discerning truth from the plethora of information available, one can cultivate good behavior and character, leading to modesty, politeness, and kindness. Virtuous individuals lead happy lives, guided by the law of truth. This key to happiness is always available to those who seek it.

Charity is a Virtue of Greatness

As human beings, we possess numerous special qualities and characteristics, but charity stands out as an exceptional one. This trait is exclusive to humans, and it elevates us above all other creatures. It is a unique strength bestowed upon us, as no other biological organism can experience the privilege of giving.

Those who give to others get huge respect. Also, the people who offered alms to Lord Mahavir were treated with respect and humility. Charity earns one name and fame that are immortal. While individuals may pass away, their charitable deeds continue to exist for generations. We honor the likes of generous donors such as Shalibhadra and Jugdushah, and the glory of Bhamasha will never fade.

A donor's name is recollected every morning, whereas being greedy is a serious character flaw that repels people. People respect and admire those who generously give to others. A generous donor is a noble soul who will undoubtedly have a human destiny again. They are the ones who feel remorseful on the days they cannot give to charity. It is widely believed that whatever you give, you receive in return, and the saying 'as you sow, so shall you reap' holds true. If we plant one seed, the earth provides us with hundreds of seeds, proving the law of giving.

It is said that beggars are our teachers who pray for alms and teach us that we may one day be in their position if we do not give alms. Therefore, charity is not only a virtue of greatness but also an essential aspect of being human.

Clarity of Goals Gives Meaning to Life

We all engage in daily activities, but the foundation of success lies in the clarity of our goals. When our goal is clear, keeping it in mind and pursuing it with determination leads to success, and this progress transforms into advancement. However, achieving our goals requires continuous effort, even in the face of challenges. Instead of accepting alternative goals, we must maintain the intensity of our pursuit to overcome hurdles and strengthen our resolve.

Achievement requires consistent practice, even after the goal is reached. Firmness towards our goals is a prerequisite for success. Changing direction midway creates mental turbulence and does not allow for stability. Before making a decision, it is essential to consider all factors. Once the decision is made, taking action with speed leads to progress and the achievement of the desired outcome.

Torky

To reach our destination, we must move in the right direction and not merely walk aimlessly. Therefore, clarity of goals provides meaning to the momentum of our endeavors.

Neither Expect Excellence nor Have Affection for the Worst

There are various events in our lives that are constantly changing, and all such events, occasions, and even the person reading or hearing them are of different qualities. If we categorize these differences into two, it would either be excellent or worst. While passing by the road, we come across many shops that draw our attention, but we only admire a few of them. We also encounter temples, hotels, and bars, and we tend to perceive temples as the best and the other places as not good.

Let us adopt a rule that neither expect excellence nor have an affection for the worst. With such a regulation, the best comes closer, and the worst disappears. If we fail to adopt this rule, the worst will enter uninvited, and it would be difficult to welcome the best. Everyone desires to achieve the best and be the best, but the question that arises is, "What is the best?" The best is the one who enriches oneself beyond sublimity.

Exploring the Topic
Neither Expect Excellence nor Have Affection for the Worst

Generally, people agree that everyone prefers the best and does not neglect it. For instance, household amenities, jewelry, garments, and tasty food - we all want the best. But why do we need to discuss this? It's because the definition of "best" is not limited to material possessions. At the worldly level, we may choose the best items, but it's not enough. We need to extend our understanding of "best" to encompass the noblest aspects of life. We can include the best books, best ideas, best thoughts, and noble individuals in our list of "best".

We can go further and think about our parents, well-wishers, friends, religious teachers, and our supreme soul as the best. However, we may not always be ready to accept these noble things when they come to us. We may even ignore them. For example, during an evening walk, a family passes by a place of worship, but the husband ignores the wife's suggestion to bow down because he had already visited it in the morning. Later, the family stops at a sugarcane juice center, and the father quickly agrees to the child's suggestion to have a glass of juice. This behavior shows how we often avoid the good and choose the ordinary. We should always follow the best and show respect.

In the past, our elders were conscious of this and would insist on respecting food and its bountiful giver. They would honor their family members' requests for tea or food before going out. This is an example of moving from the physical to the spiritual level. If you find it challenging to follow this, you should feel pain. It must hurt to fail to progress for the better at every step. If you are too involved in the mundane and worse things, it can obstruct your path to uttam.

Sometimes circumstances or karma can drive us away, but we should not choose this path. We have been granted better means and materials, so the final result should be the best one.

Preventing Waste is Essential in Resource Scarcity

Imagine a scorching summer day in a village, where water is only supplied once a day for a mere thirty minutes. In this situation, everyone prepares their buckets and vessels well in advance, following all the rules attentively. Similarly, in a desert region like 'Bhal', people know that water is precious and must be reserved only for drinking, as it is often sourced from far distances. This awareness of rarity helps prevent waste and ensures that resources are used wisely.

Likewise, our human birth is a rare and precious opportunity, granted to only a select few beings for a short span after infinite rebirths. Therefore, it is not a time to relax, but a time to raise our virtues and to take action through doing good deeds. By spreading positivity and using our time and resources wisely, we can help prevent waste and make the most of this precious gift. Remember, awareness of rarity prevents wastage.

સંયમ એ યમનો પણ યમ છે

Self-restraint for prosperity

A city or town is often surrounded by a fort, which serves as a shield of protection for all citizens. This fort must be exceptionally strong and have entry and exit doors, as well as guards to ensure that no harmful elements enter. Even the smallest crack or hole in the fort must be immediately repaired, as its strength is essential to its safety.

The analogy of the fort extends to our own lives. Just as a fort protects citizens, we must protect our own body, mind, and life to achieve gradual prosperity. This protection requires restraint to prevent harmful elements from tarnishing our inner sanctity. We must control our instincts and activities to maintain a genuine and prosperous life.

To achieve this, we must make a resolution to build a sturdy wall around ourselves, which we can call the "wall-pledge-rule." By establishing strong regulations, we can secure our inner beauty and maintain a clear

and spotless life. An old proverb states that "A bull is useless without a master," and similarly, a person without rules is worthless. Therefore, we must all voluntarily commit to making our body, mind, and life clean, healthy, resistant, and simple.

मित्ति मे सव्वभूएसु

My Friendship is with All Living Beings

My friendship is with all living beings is a powerful statement that embodies the teachings of Lord Mahavir, a source of inspiration for many. His life was full of extraordinary events that continue to inspire people to this day. One such event was when he entered a forest to enlighten a cobra named Chandkaushik, who had blinded himself with rage and bitten the Lord's toe, injecting all his venom. Lord Mahavir cast a gentle glance of compassion and spoke the words, "Bujh bujh Chandkaushiya," which means, "Understand Chandkaushik and realize what you are doing." When the cobra met the Lord's gaze, he felt a wave of peace and tranquility engulf his inner self. He suddenly visualized his previous births, an experience known as Jatismaran-Gyan. Chandkaushik retreated to his hole and fasted until death. Lord Mahavir stood there for a fortnight, protecting his virtues, sentiments, and affinity, just as a doctor observes a patient after surgery.

The nature of helping others and doing good deeds enhances life, and sowing the seed of philanthropy is a form of self-improvement. The extension of compassion is the motivating factor behind benevolence and obligation.

Whether it's Diwali or Not, Keep the Lamp Lit

Once again, Diwali has arrived with a message for those who are willing to listen. The message is simple but profound: once you light the lamp, let it shine brightly.

There is a deeper meaning hidden between these words. The lighting of the lamp is a symbol of the light within ourselves. Just as the lamp illuminates everything around it, our presence should also light up the hearts of those around us. This is what relationships are all about. Who doesn't need friends and family? It's impossible to survive without a social life. As social creatures, we need connections with others. We should cherish the precious relationships we have with the people in our lives, and maintain the bonds we've established in the past.

As we celebrate the new year, let us make sure that our relationships continue to shine like the sparkling lamps of Diwali. Let us be mindful and make sure that the light of our connections doesn't fade or extinguish.

He Who Knows Where to Stop, Doesn't Face Disasters

Proverbs have been handed down through the ages, preserving the wisdom of our ancestors. Each time we encounter a proverb, it can reveal new meanings depending on the context, the person, and the time. Imagine you're enjoying a delicious meal, but before you know it, you've eaten way too much. This is where the proverb "He who knows where to stop, don't face disasters" comes in handy. By being mindful of how much we eat, we can prevent overindulgence and the accompanying health risks. It is a common saying in Sanskrit "रसमूलानि व्याधयः॥", it means that the cause of disease is attachment towards flavor.

This proverb applies not only to eating but also to spending money and conducting business. If we know when to stop, we can prevent many problems and avoid conflicts. The key is to develop a sense of discrimination, which can help us recognize our limits. Let us always keep this lamp of wisdom burning!

Bridging the Gap Between Understanding and Behavior

Let's explore the relationship between understanding and behavior. We need to pay attention to which one prevails and when: understanding or behavior?

People can perceive our understanding from our words, gestures, and writings in each moment, while our nature is evident in our day-to-day behavior. Our behavior reflects our temperament, while our communication represents our understanding. When there is a conflict between the two, our nature takes over and understanding fades away. Genuine understanding means being able to control our temperament. Therefore, a change in our temperament is the fruit of our comprehensive understanding. Knowledge is the key to understanding, and it brings wisdom. Knowledge is like a mirror that helps us to beautify ourselves. As we gain knowledge, our behavior improves, and our understanding enhances the beauty of our nature, making us more transparent.

Escher

The closer our behavior aligns with our understanding, the better we become.

Importance of Building a Strong Personal Identity

You may have come across a well-written letter or message delivered by the post office. In such cases, a clearly written address is crucial. The same principle applies to human beings as well - a clumsily written address does not reach its intended destination. Our character is our true address or identity. People will judge you by your character alone. There is no substitute for a good character. No shortcuts, no excuses. In the old days, we used to hear remarks like, "This gentleman would never do wrong. He would not use foul language or eat anything inappropriate." There was a strong sense of trust in those golden times.

However, things have changed today. We often hear people say, "Oh, I can't trust him; he can do anything." But we must remember that it's up to us to build our character. Are you working somewhere? Be honest. Running your own business? Don't be rude. Have you been entrusted with responsibilities? Don't cheat. When we are not driven by fear or greed, we can earn respect and praise from everyone. Let us strive to build such a character.

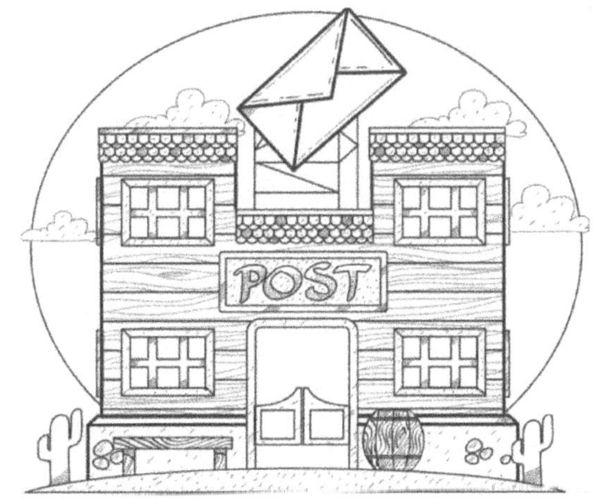

દોષો માટીપગા છે, ગુણો હાથીપગા છે.

Vice is Dust, Virtue is Gold!

Human beings often suffer from vices such as lust, anger, greed, and desire. Many people accept these vices as universal traits and convince themselves that they cannot be changed. However, if you think seriously about it, you will realize that these vices are weaknesses and losses. One need not be discouraged, as these vices are temporary and will vanish.

There are examples to support this belief. For instance, Chandkoshi was once terribly furious, but he eventually became docile and felt sorry for his actions. Similarly, Bhavdev had immense attraction for Nagila, but when he became Jambuswami, all his delusions were wiped out, and he became a significant example of non-attachment.

Rather than fighting against vices, it is better to neglect them and execute their counterforce. For instance, one should follow forgiveness to counter anger and non-attachment to counter attachment. Finding the opposite of a particular vice and following it is one way to defeat that vice, as it is like battling from one end and facing it bravely from the other end. This is why we exist on this earth. Let us start!

Good Resolutions are Like Wish-Fulfilling Trees

What you believe in your mind is likely to manifest in your outer world. Our inner world is a fertile ground, and whatever we plant will grow. Therefore, we should always strive to plant good seeds. Good resolutions are like wish-fulfilling trees that bloom with positive outcomes.

It only takes one resolution to start the process. However, we must nurture it constantly for it to succeed. Even a hard stone can become scarce if it is rubbed repeatedly. Thus, the key to success is to be steadfast and resolute. Be patient, remind yourself of your resolution, and persevere for a long time. By doing so, you will reap the rewards.

Just like adding a drop of curd to milk turns the whole milk into curd, taking a good resolution with full sincerity and commitment will undoubtedly lead to success.

Maximizing Blessings by Developing Your Competence

When we pray to the Almighty and don't receive an answer, we sometimes begin to doubt God. Instead of doing that, we should examine our own competence. If we do this, we will realize that we get what we deserve. If we sharpen our skills and qualifications, we will receive rewards that are just as good.

Consider the river Ganga, which has an endless flow of water. It can quench our thirst, but we can only fill our containers up to their capacity. If we want more, we must increase our own capacity. Similarly, if we want to be blessed by Parmatma, we must first make ourselves worthy. We must constantly deepen and widen our virtues so that we can receive Parmatma's blessings. The Almighty has a standing offer, which we should not miss. The only condition is that we must strike a balance between his generosity and our capacity.

The Power and Pitfalls of Comparison

Consider the trickiness of comparison. I was once feeling happy, even important, when suddenly a comparison with someone else crossed my mind. A tingle ran through my fingertips as my happiness vanished and bitterness filled my heart. But then, someone reminded me of a very unlucky situation, and I felt happy that someone else was more unhappy than me. What is this power of comparison?

In another instance, a gentleman was enjoying a funfair. He walked enthusiastically, happily singing. Along the way, he saw many people wearing shoes and felt sorry for himself, as he was barefoot. He was unable to walk any further and became upset. However, he managed to drag himself a few more steps and saw a lame, crippled man lying on a wheelbarrow. He thought to himself, "oh, he has no legs. Thank God I have legs." He smiled and his sorrows disappeared. Our joys and sorrows depend on comparison.

The point to ponder is that we should feel happiness or sadness without comparing ourselves to others. Our burdens and troubles result from comparison, and our

joys and sorrows are not real. We must free ourselves from this habit. Furthermore, when we label someone as good or bad, we do it by comparison. Let us be free of the comparison complex and think of reality.

ततः किम्?

So What?

The mantra "Tat-Kim"('so what') is believed to have a powerful and miraculous effect similar to an antidote to venomous bites, such  as those from snakes or scorpions. The phrase "So What?" is a powerful tool that can help alleviate negative thoughts. Our thoughts can bring us joy or sadness, as we may think of others wealth, status, and fame and feel that we are lacking in these areas. This can lead to feelings of unhappiness and inferiority. However, if we think "So What?" in such moments, we can remind ourselves that others' fortune is not ours, and we may receive these things in the future if we deserve them.

Moreover, even if we do receive fame and fortune, we should remember the phrase "So What?" to remind ourselves that such things are temporary and ultimately meaningless. This mantra can help us overcome our ego and gain a new perspective on life. By believing in "So What?", we can see through the temptation of worldly wealth and status.

These two simple words have a deep meaning, and thinking about them can help us find solutions to our problems.

Let Your Heart Beat with Empathy

The current era is often referred to as the age of machines. While we have greatly benefited from it, there are also several drawbacks. Our lives have become intertwined with gadgets such as phones, computers,

and televisions, resulting in a mechanical lifestyle. Although our brains think, our hearts feel, it is important to maintain sensitivity.

When something becomes a part of our daily routine, it can kill our sensitivity. In the past, people had a strong connection with animals when they used to ride horses, use bullock carts, and till the land with bulls. They had love and sympathy for animals, and they thought about their joy and sorrow. This sensitivity was an integral part of our lives and made our existence more sensitive to the natural world.

Sensitivity is a treasure of life, and we must maintain it by all means. It is the source of all our arts, including music, painting, sculptures, and so on. The ability to appreciate fine arts is a gift from our sensitivity that allows us to feel and enjoy beautiful things, ultimately leading to inner wealth and conscience development.

Sensitivity makes us sad when we see others unhappy, and we feel others' pain as our own. However, we are now at risk of losing this sensitivity. It is time to regain it. We must fill our hearts with love, tenderness, sympathy, and sensitivity. We need to spend more time in nature, such as among trees, flowers, forests, valleys, and mountains. The sun, moon, and stars can also be our companions. We should also spend time with small children to develop a soft and sensitive heart.

Appreciating Beauty in Simplicity

If you ever find yourself at Prabhas Patan's seashore, you will be awe-struck by the magnificent view of Somnath Mahadev Temple. Its stunning architecture is flawless, but what adds to its beauty

is the emptiness surrounding it. The temple stands majestically with no constructions around it, and the Indian ocean flows at its feet, stretching up to the horizon, leaving nothing to obstruct the view. The vastness of the environs is charming enough to leave a lasting impression.

Imagine a big house with no other constructions around it; it would be very attractive. However, if it were surrounded by other constructions, its beauty would be overshadowed, and its charm would be lost. Similarly, if you attend an exciting event followed by another event, your experience of the former event will be diminished.

You read a great book; close your eyes and sit silently, ponder over the best chapter, absorbing its ideas. Savor it. Beauty born out of inner thoughts and feelings will leave a lasting impression and its impact will remain forever. Similarly, when you eat delicious food, stop, and savor the first and the best bite. The taste of food remains etched in memory. Do not fill up too much, leaving some space.

In short, to enjoy the good things in life, we need to leave space. The reason for the beauty of a good painting is the empty space surrounding the main object. Leaving blank space is an essential part of its composition to make it more attractive. Too much of anything creates a mess, and mess is always untidy. All good things in life need space to be what they are. Let us learn from the art of leaving blank space. Remember, everything in excess is poison. Do not be overburdened and overcrowded. Presently, we are suffering from the excess mania. It is a disease. Save yourself and be happy!

Sorrow Demands Reflection, Not Projection

Paryushan is a unique festival that stands out among all other parvas. It is important to engage in pratikraman (penitential retreat), fasting, and other penances during Paryushan, as well as listening to the Kalpasutra. The story of Lord Indra and Kartik Sheth is told in the very first address of the Kalpasutra, and many of us are familiar with it. The event of Tapas in the Kalpasutra is also well-known to us. The mirror parable of Gairik Tapas is full of wisdom, and if we understand it, we can eliminate sorrowful or painful experiences from our lives.

Gairik Tapas insisted that he would break his fast only with the hands of Kartik Sheth. The king asked Kartik Sheth to come for the fast-breaking ceremony of Gairik, but at that moment, Gairik insulted Kartik Sheth in front of everyone by putting his fingers on his nose. Kartik Sheth could have blamed the king and Gairik and retorted, but instead, he calmly thought about himself. He reflected on why this had happened to him, and his thought was not in vain. It was very thought-provoking: "Had I been initiated by the worthy hands of Munisuvrat Swami, this insulting incident would not have happened to all." Thus, in the time of sorrow, he did not use binoculars to see what others had done but used a mirror to see himself and his own faults.

This incident shows that whenever negative things happen, we must reflect on our duty and our right approach and attitude. Why blame others? Why decide what others should do? Such thinking is negative and unproductive. The real solution lies in self-analysis. Thus, we should rely on a mirror rather than binoculars. During the holy days of Paryushan, let us determine that in times of sorrow and distress, we will look into the mirror. We will see what we should do, and we will improve our actions and attitude.

Love is a Serene Symphony, But Expectations are the Dissonant Notes

Our minds are complex and can contain both positivity and negativity, kindness and selfishness, and these contradictory elements can grow simultaneously without interruption. It's similar to roses with sharp thorns. Is there a way to enjoy the fragrance of the roses while avoiding the thorns? It should be considered an art to do so, but it's possible to acquire. It's a common experience that loving sincerely brings happiness and satisfaction, whether it's towards humans, birds, or animals. Love brings happiness to both the giver and the receiver.

However, if our love is like a rose with thorns, then the thorns are our expectations, which can invite sorrow and shock. Sometimes, our expectations multiply, and we are never satisfied. This can be painful and gradually diminish the happiness of love. The only solution is to love fully without expectations, to make friendship and affection our symphony while being alert and away from

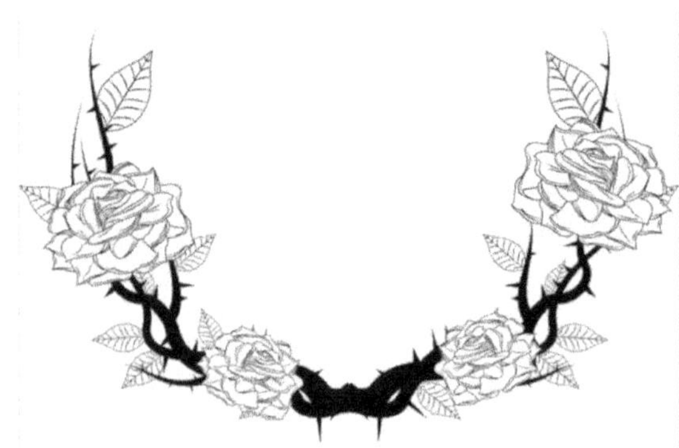

expectations. We want nothing in return. If we do this, we can have the nectar of love and honey of the lover at all times without sorrow and shock.

Initially, this may seem difficult, but it's essential to be determined and practice. Once we succeed, our lives can touch the sky with glory.

Let's do it!

The Perils of Overindulgence

In the modern era, houses are built using bricks and cement. Two bricks are joined by cement, which is bonded by water. Without water, this bond is not possible, but if there is too much water, it will not combine the cement and the bricks. The amount of water used should be proportionate. Similarly, a flowering plant, a fruit-bearing tree, and seeds waiting to grow need water with soil, but the quantity of water must be moderate. Water gives life to plants, but too much water will cause them to wither. Therefore, balance is required in every aspect of life. Unfortunately, excess seems to be flourishing everywhere nowadays. We can see this in our marriage functions, children's get-togethers, or any social event. Excessive parental affection can also be harmful.

The proverb "proportionate poison is medicine while excess of hector is poison" sends a message that avoiding excess is important. We need to be alert and let prudence guide us, to be wise in all areas of life.

અધૂરપ ઢાંકીએ - સારપ ઉપસાવીએ

Cover Shortcomings and Embrace Goodness

A person was sitting on the outskirts of a dense forest, wanting to cross it but unable to do so because of their lameness. Just then, a blind man approached with the same intention but couldn't navigate the forest without sight. Despite their disabilities, they both resolved to overcome their problem through cooperation. The blind man carried the lame one on his shoulders, and the latter guided him through the forest with their vision. Together, they happily crossed the forest, proving that unity of goodness can overcome shortcomings.

Dual relationships, such as father-son, brother-brother, husband-wife, and guru-disciple, also contain both shortcomings and goodness. These pairs complement each other, covering each other's imperfections to accomplish tasks. The human condition encompasses both shortcomings and goodness; one can never find one without the other. Therefore, it is crucial to accept and appreciate the positive sides of others,

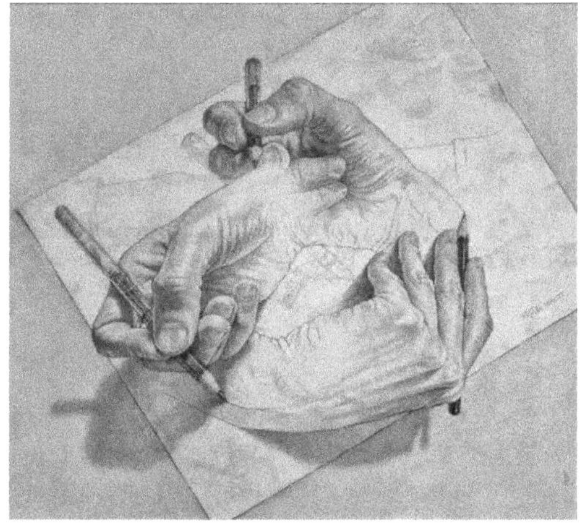

Oriol Angrill

connecting your goodness with theirs to live a happy life. Do not focus on others' shortcomings; instead, recognize their strengths and unite them with your own to create a fruitful relationship.

Internal Silence is God's Throne

The meaning of words is limited, but the meaning of silence is infinite. There is silence before the words and there is silence after. However, if silence is expressive, its value decreases. If silence is accompanied by wisdom, its beauty is enhanced. When words fail to convey our message, silence can often succeed and help us. The impact of silence can be more powerful than words. Let us observe ourselves. Many times, we regret speaking and wish we had remained quiet. Such lists of regrets can be long. It is rare that we feel that speaking would have been better.

Speaking requires intelligence, and the same is true for silence. When you speak, you must be conscious of what to say, when to say it, where to say it, and how much to say. However, silence requires nothing but wisdom.

People consider those who speak little are more reliable and trustworthy than those who are talkative. Silence itself is effective and impressive. On the contrary, words require silence to be meaningful. Silence is self-illuminating and self-sufficient. It saves and treasures your energy. Of course, both words and silence are important in their own ways. To be strong, one needs to develop the silence of words. The next step is the silence of thoughts. Keep gaps (silence) between one thought and the next. This will enlighten you. Such silence of thoughts allows you to enrich your supremacy. Let us welcome the best with silence!

Curiosity Makes You Scholar

If you ask a question, you only reveal your ignorance once. However, if you do not ask, you remain ignorant forever. So, it's essential to ask questions, inquire, and be curious to clear your doubts. If the respondent has the knowledge, they can definitely help clear your doubts. Being superficially smart can lead to foolishness if you try to avoid asking questions. Thus, we must strive to be free from doubt, and our goal should be to have a clear mind. That's why people say that asking more questions can make you a scholar. Both the one who asks and the one who answers the questions are praiseworthy.

Spiritual soul Shri Anand-Ghanji rightly said "ધન્ય તું આતમા જેહને એહવો પ્રશ્ન અવકાશ રે!", "Praise the soul who ask these kinds of questions." When someone asked Shri Anand-Ghanji about the meaning of internal peace and how one can know their mind, he praised him with the above quote and answered with great blessings.

Everyone is curious and has questions and queries. Who wouldn't have questions? The answer is that only the Supreme Almighty or someone who is completely ignorant would not have any questions. We are in between these two extremes, so we should ask philosophical questions rather than just curiosity-based questions. Asking philosophical queries can lead us to ultimate knowledge.

What Else is There to Do? Yes, There is Something Meaningful to Do

During a public speech, a renowned poet and speaker shared an incident he witnessed while riding a rickshaw at 9 o'clock in the morning in Vallabh-vidya Nagar. He saw two young boys quarrelling and pulling each other's shirts, appearing furious and angry. He decided to intervene and asked them to stop  fighting and go their separate ways, as it was not the proper thing to do. However, one of the boys responded, "what else is there to do?"

Dhruv Kumar, the speaker, quickly came up with a solution. He took both boys in his rickshaw and employed them with the task of sweeping and cleaning the compound. This made them calm down and slowly but surely everything became alright.

Upon hearing this incident, I reflected on how many people waste their time on meaningless activities and pass their lives in vain. I feel pity for them and repeated the boy's question, "What else to do?"

The solution is to find the best books and associates that can help you achieve your goals. Eating and drinking should not be the focus of life. Instead, we should involve ourselves in helping others, developing virtues, or pursuing interests like music, painting, or spirituality. This higher goal will lead us to a better and more fulfilling life. Without such a goal, life has no meaning. Human life is not meant for idle pursuits or senseless activities. We must strive to make it meaningful.

I encourage the audience to get inspired by reading biographies of exemplary individuals, to follow their examples, and aim for higher goals. Living a virtuous and sensible life will bring fulfillment and purpose.

પ્રસાર પામો શુભ-લાભ વાતો!
Let's Spread Good Messages

We start using warm blankets when the cold weather sets in. Similarly, when there's a fire, we run in search of water to protect ourselves. We accumulate counter equipment to safeguard ourselves against such situations.

There's a great need for auspicious elements as evil is troubling us. Probably never before has there been such an urgent need for such elements in the cycle of life.

There are many uninvited causes around us that disturb us. Let's stimulate the good seeds inside us and neglect the evil. It's especially important to tell moral and value-added stories to young children at bedtime. Such communication is crucial for their future and the development of good character. Positive thoughts should be nurtured from the beginning. This is the first and foremost duty of all wise parents.

There are a few lines in my mind leading to the following things - should I utter them? Lend me your ears!

May goodness and courage reign in each abode,
Where every child is a noble crown to behold,
With right conduct and positivity that glows,
They shall be the glory of our nation's mold.

Footprints on the Sand of Time

When faced with the choice of saving either money or reputation, a wise person would choose to safeguard their reputation over their wealth, house, or jewelry. They understand that possessions are fleeting and can easily be lost or regained, but a damaged reputation is much harder to recover. Wealth may come and go, but one's reputation and goodwill should be protected at all costs, even if it means giving up material possessions.

It is important to prioritize wisely, giving up "little" for "many," and never sacrificing "much" for "little." While money can bring temporary status, it is one's character, virtues and generosity that leave a lasting impression on others. People who possess these qualities are always remembered fondly, long after their wealth has been forgotten.

Prestige and fame are not just desirable, but essential components of a truly valuable life. Simply existing is not enough; it is only when we live with good character and reputation that we truly achieve greatness. Our name and reputation will be remembered long after our money and possessions have disappeared, leaving footprints in the sands of time.

A Loving Relationship is a Creation of the Heart

Connection is the foundation of a society. It becomes difficult to live without it in a society. Relationships are a more concrete version of connection. The core of a relationship is love. Just as we need cement to build a dam which stores river water, love is required to guide the positive emotions flowing from the heart and build meaningful relationships. Love is a product of the heart, not the intellect.

When the calculation of the mind begins, the boundaries of affection become narrower, and the history of the relationship approaches its end, decreasing duration of the relationship. Whether the relationship is with a relative like a brother, father, or friend, or with a community, sweetness disappears, and the relationship becomes like artificial flowers, with practical but temporary existence.

However, those who embrace the emotions bursting from the abyss of the heart erase geographical boundaries and reserve a place in history. These relationships are kept alive through the exchange of affection.

The first lesson is to stay dedicated and generous, like a tree that only gives. It produces flowers and fruits in all seasons and follows the motto to grow and give. Building, developing, and beautifying relationships require this type of dedication. There is a business outside of mathematics, and it is the cultivation of love and affection."

सख्खा परम दुल्हा

The scriptures of Uttradhyayan and the scholars have explicitly mentioned that the only purpose of the soul is to practice Dharma, which is the right faith. Shree Uttradhyayanji mentions four precious things, but faith is considered the rarest gem. It is obtained by oneself and cannot be borrowed like other things. Faith is your inner strength and the more you have it, the better the results. Faith grows within you, and it requires care, nurture, and

nourishment. Doubt and misinterpretation can kill faith, so be cautious. Ordinary beings have not realized its power, but those who have realized it never waver or become unsteady. They follow their gurus and gain miraculous rewards in return.

An example of the power of faith is the lamp being lit by the water of holy Shatrunjay. Bharwad witnessed this miracle and narrated it to us. Faith is the main factor in miracles. Sometimes, we are misguided to accept our belief as faith, but it is not. Belief and faith may look similar, but this resemblance is deceptive. It is important to draw a line of demarcation and realize that the most precious element is faith.

A Speech that Embraces Multiple Viewpoints

Here is a short fable for good readers. In a dense forest near a pond, a lion was drinking water when a tiger arrived and joined him. After quenching their thirst, they began to converse. It was the month of February, and the cold breeze was blowing. The lion said, "It is cold because it is the month of March."  The tiger disagreed and said, "It's expected to be cold in February, so it must be February." The debate could have gone on indefinitely, but the lion suggested asking a fox who was coming from the opposite direction.

The poor fox was terrified because two wild creatures were focusing on him, but he was clever. The tiger asked him if it was cold in February, and the lion asked if it was cold in March. The fox was confused and didn't want to displease either of them, but he was astute enough to say that, 

माघे वा फाल्गुने वापि शीतं वहति मारुतः |
तदा शीतं विजानीयाद् न माघे न च फ़ाल्गुने ||

મહા કે ફાગણમાં, જ્યારે ઠંડી ઠંડી હવા વહે
શિયાળો જાણવો ત્યારે, ન માહે નહીં ફાગણે

When the breeze is cool and free,
Winter's presence we should see,
Not just in February or March,
But whenever cold becomes our parch.

The fox's smart response is thought-provoking because it is close to the truth. The language of the fox in this fable is the language of Lord Mahavir.

Prabhu Mahavir spoke the language of Anekant (looking at things from all angles). Rather than seeing things in a binary and simplistic manner, we should strive to consider different perspectives. We should accept ideas with an open mind and never be imprisoned by our own opinions. Try to understand all possible truths free from any particular angle. We should understand and embrace the pervasive truth that is not bound by any boundaries.

Vihar: The Journey of Self-Discovery Amidst the Wonders of Nature

Vihar, which means journey of a monk, is not just walking. It is a journey free from bondages, without doors or windows, just walking under the sky on the earth. Wide hovering clouds, vast earth to walk upon, and fresh air everywhere create a positive atmosphere. The birds chirping, animals moving, and humans thinking in this peaceful environment is a joyous experience. The clear sky, tall trees, clean waterfalls, and cool breeze of spring season provide new vision and fresh thoughts.

In the midst of nature, your conscience recharges, reminding me of a prayer in Vedas: "आ नो भद्राः क्रतवो यन्तु विश्वतः" (Aano Bhadra, krtavo yantu vishwatah), which means, "let all the good thoughts come to us from all directions." We should reflect on this shloka.

In the peaceful and silent caves of Himalayas, even a single positive thought can spread everywhere. We should be ready to welcome it and make it our own. In my own experience, this journey is a process to

explore oneself. It is a treasure that leads to mental and scientific growth and brings delightful blissful pleasure that uplifts the soul and enlightens you.

Only those who have experienced such a vihar can understand the beauty of it.

A Clean Background is Essential for a Beautiful Painting

In present times, it is surprising to see the multitude of religious rituals. If we were to count them, it would surely exceed our expectations. However, the paradox lies in the fact that despite the high number of rituals, morality seems to have declined. This disparity warrants serious investigation. If we carefully analyze and observe it, we will realize that conducting rituals is often incomplete and disorderly, lacking a clean foundation. Essentially, it is akin to harvesting without planting the seeds. How can one expect crops to grow in such circumstances?

Imagine a painter with colors, brushes, imagination, and the willingness to create a masterpiece. But the canvas or wall on which he must paint is dirty. In such a scenario, the painter cannot create his best work. A clean background is a fundamental requirement for a beautiful and eye-pleasing painting. The clarity of the wall enhances the impact of the picture.

Similarly, excellent religious rituals require a clean and pure mindset. The absence of envy, cheapness, and impurity is a must. To make religious rituals worthwhile, one needs purity, simplicity, faith, compassion, and love to enrich them. All rituals should lead one towards salvation rather than merely be a mode of action.

ये दिन भी बीत जायेगा

This Too Shall Pass

We come across many sentences each day. Some sentences are such that they never get rusty or old, never become outdated, and never feel irrelevant. Different meanings flow from them all the time. If your mind is numb, unwanted thoughts rush in, and you might feel like ending your life. But when the wind of meaningful sentences blows, dark clouds of such thoughts disperse and the whole sky becomes clean. How wonderful it is!

Just like people with diabetes or heart disease keep life-saving medicines in their pockets, keeping small cards with meaningful sentences in your wallet is equally useful. When you see someone's wealth and feel envy and anxiety, just take out the card and read: "If my virtue awakens, I will get the same. Let that person be happy." With the help of these cards, negative thoughts disappear.

Feeling disgusted or angry at someone? Remove the card that reads: "सव्वे जीवा कम्मवस ।" "All beings are acting according to their own karma." Such a thought will change your focus and redirect your anger towards karma instead of the person.

If you're dealing with a disease, take out the card that reads: "Anything that comes, comes to go. This too shall pass." Remember that diseases are rampant, and even if only one or two have appeared, it's the grace of God.

Are you a victim of inferiority complex? Just think: "I am physically fit and wealthy; my parents and family were happy with my birth." Remove the card and read: "उजाले अपनी यादों का हमारे साथ रहने दो। न जाने किस गलीमें शाम ढल जाये ।।" "Let the brightness of your memories stay with us, who knows where the evening might pass."

Start making cards with such meaningful sentences and keep them close to your heart. It is a wonderful way to maintain your perspective even in the face of adversity. If you want a happy life and a smiling face, this is the best advice!

The Lamp of Wisdom: A Shield Against Dark Thoughts

A happy mind is a wish fulfilling tree. When our minds are filled with joy, all our sufferings seem bearable, and happiness becomes worth spreading. We have all experienced this feeling before. The question is, when is the mind happy?

The answer is that the mind is happy when instincts of anger, ego, and other negative emotions weaken, and a natural wave of happiness rises within the mind. However, this wave of happiness often dissipates due to destructive ideas that come from outside or even from within. To combat these defeating thoughts, a large army of defensive thoughts needs to be on alert at their arrival. At the same time, the lamp of wisdom should be lit within us, so that we clearly see that these thoughts are killing our happiness. With the help of wisdom, we can keep our minds away from such thoughts, so that our minds become subservient to positive thoughts and inactive in unworthy deeds.

A fierce battle raged between two brothers, Bahubali and Bharat. Bahubali's ego was hurt when Bharat held the chakraratna (a miracle wheel used as a weapon). A roar arose in Bahubali, "Where do I lack? How dare he unleash his chakra on me? My mighty fist is enough to smash my brother."

At that moment, Bahubali's instinctive mind awakened, and he became angry. However, as soon as the happiness of his mind met with ego and anger, joy vanished, and the potential for violence appeared.

As Bahubali raised his hand, the light of wisdom lamp rose, giving him clarity. His anger turned to respect. He realized, "How can I kill my own brother? How can I attempt such a disrespectful act?" At that moment, he changed his mind. Instead of lowering his hand to hit his brother, he used it to pluck his hair as a symbol of giving up everything and renouncing the worldly life. Bahubali became a sage, and there was no anger within him anymore.

This type of defensive thinking allows the plant of happiness to blossom and grow, never to fade away. The moment that anger and ego tendencies start destroying happiness, we must form the fence of opposite thoughts to protect the plant of happiness.

The Sunrise is on the Other Side of the Wall

It is a fact that the entire universe can brighten with thousands of streaks of light emitting from within us. But why isn't it visible to us? What thick cover is blocking it? The answer to this question will only appear when we let go of our efforts to see it.

Our body is itself the first layer. Adjacent to it is an impenetrable wall that is the citadel of our senses. Next is what we call "mind," which is as hard as a thunderbolt and serves as a barricade. If we can penetrate both the front and back layers of this wall, only a small hole is enough to brighten the entire universe. Human birth is the only opportunity to penetrate and cross this wall. We can find motivation from those

who have succeeded in this seemingly inaccessible task and learn from their experiences of opening the door and experiencing the bliss of light. We must believe that such a destination exists. Indeed, everyone's way is different!

Even the lines of this couplet point to a good path:

આભમાં કે દરિયામાં, ક્યાંય પણ કેડી નથી;
અર્થ એનો એ નથી કે, કોઈએ સફર ખેડી નથી

No trails in sky or ocean wide,
doesn't mean none have ever tried.
Journeys made, though not well-known,
Paths discovered by those alone.

(by poet Rajesh Vyas).

Let us surrender completely. A shower of victory awaits!

Showing Right Direction to Astray

In today's world, many people struggle to find meaning in their lives. It seems that our minds have lost their sense of direction. When we walk in the wrong direction, we cannot reach our destination. For instance, if we want to reach a village to the west, but we head east instead, we won't get there.

Indians are known for their emotional and heartfelt nature. They value bonds and relationships. However, when a person starts living solely for material wealth, status, and prosperity, we must ask ourselves, "What about the progress and quality of life?"

Indian people are nurtured by love, compassion, warmth, and emotions, which are essential for our survival. How can we walk comfortably on the path of intelligence and wealth when our emotions disappear as we focus more on our minds and money? Material possessions such as jewelry and lavish clothes can become a burden for a body without a soul. Even the most charming beauty can lose its appeal.

We, who are in search of happiness are akin to a musk deer, constantly jumping from one desire to another. We must eventually break free from intoxication of mind and money, and search for real happiness through sharing love and affection. Whatever we give to others, we receive back in double or more. The highway towards happiness lies in the act of giving.

Rather than being impatient and distressed, we should relax and seek peace. This inner peace will reflect in our soul and make it shine. We will find peace, love, and joy in our hearts. This is our true necessity, and this is the only way to true happiness.

॥ कः सुखी, कः सुखी, कः सुखी ॥

In today's world, a sizable number of people are seeking happiness. They all have a longing to be the happiest person in the universe. From one point of view, people today seem to have everything they need to be happy - material possessions, luxury, and comfort. And yet, they still lack happiness. It's like a thirsty fish in the middle of the ocean. All these material possessions are only useful for physical pleasure, but what about mental peace? The mind is unpleasant, unhappy, and unpeaceful.

If you want to get rid of this feeling, the secret lies in your hands - love everyone unconditionally. Shower abundant love on all, and happiness will naturally come to you. The foundation of love is friendliness. Without love, there can't be friendliness. If your heart overflows with love, it will reflect in your eyes as well. When love flows through your vision, you become unaware of others' faults. If you don't see anyone's faults, you won't have aversion. Aversion comes along with disrespect, attitude, rejection, and aggression. If we don't welcome aversion towards any human, happiness floods all around.

If we visualize aversion in all beings, we will only notice hatred, and hatred welcomes unhappiness. However, if our vision is full of compassion, then our hearts will play a melodious tune of happiness.

So, love everyone unconditionally, and let happiness be your companion.

"Kalyan thavo vishwa nu!"

www.ingramcontent.com/pod-product-compliance
Lightning Source LLC
Chambersburg PA
CBHW042101150726
48005CB00033B/1507